FOR HIS SALVATION

VOLUME 1

For His Salvation
Copyright © 2023 by Kendryana Scharschmidt
All rights reserved.

No part of this book may be reproduced or used in any manner without the prior written permission of the copyright owner, except for the use of brief quotations in a book review.

Disclaimer

Scripture quotation marked ESV are taken from the ESV® Bible (The Holy Bible English Standard Version®).

Copyright © 2001 by Crossway, publishing ministry of Good News Publishers. Used by permission. All rights reserved.

Scripture quotations marked NLT are taken from the Holy Bible, New Living Translation. © 1996, 2004, 2007, 2013 by Tyndale House Foundation. Used by permission of Tyndale House Publishers Inc., Carol Stream, Illinois 60188. All rights reserved.

Scripture quotations marked KJV are taken from the King James Bible Version of the Bible.

License Notes This book and eBook is licensed for your personal enjoyment only. This book and eBook may not be re-sold or given away to other people. If you would like to share this book with another person, please purchase an additional copy for each PERSON, you share it with. Thank you for respecting the hard work of this author. No part of this publication may be reproduced, distributed, or transmitted in any form or by any means, including photocopying, recording, or other electronic or mechanical methods, without the prior written permission of the publisher, except in the case of brief quotations embodied in critical reviews and certain other non-commercial uses permitted by copyright law.

Cover Design by Kendryana Scharschmidt
Publisher's Name Kendryana Scharschmidt

Table of Contents

Introduction-
- For God So Loved the World

In The Beginning- Page 9
-Side Note- page 13-17

Test and Trials- Page 46

The Wait- Page-60
-My Husband- Page -75
-A Wife- Page 77
-Trust The Process- Page -93

To Be Continued- Page 97

For GOD'S love for man was so great that
HE endured,
all pain.

In The Beginning

Tuesday May 28th, 2019
5:37am-morning

God told me that my husband was going to cheat on me in "half a semester" I believe that's going to be 6 months. I'm scared, I LOVE MY HUSBAND. God said he loves me too.

So, I asked, "Why is this happening?"
GOD said, He needed my husband to call on Him. I asked GOD, "Will I know when it happens?" He said "no, not leading up to it, but once it's done, I will know."

God told me not to ask him about it right away, because he will lie. I asked God, "How will in know?" I heard Him say, "I will show you." I'm not sure what that means!

How DO I Feel!!??
I'm scared, I want to turn over and slap the mess out of him in his sleep. I want to cry all night; I want a Divorce.

I don't want him to hurt me again, God, I really can't take it. I would not do this to him, I love him. I also feel disgusted that I am 3 months pregnant, and my husband is going to give himself to somebody else. He's going to take advantage of me.
GOD told me I'm having a baby (boy?)

Side Note

You may be wondering wait what, all of this so suddenly? Good! Because that's exactly what I felt after that night. My heart was beating fast, and I had sweated out my silk press. I had awakened from a dream of my husband and this woman, and I knew he had cheated on me with her, he denied it at first but in my soul, I knew it. When I woke up, I heard GOD speak in my mind. It was like I was having a conversation with Him. I had never experienced that before. I asked Him was my husband going to cheat on me, and He said yes.

Every good thing about my marriage turned bad. All the love I had for my husband turned into bitterness. All the time we should've been rejoicing I was mourning, and my husband never knew it. The rest of my pregnancy I was depressed, and my life turned upside down, from one bad dream and one encounter with GOD.

Okay you may say that could have been just one bad dream! No! This was different. There was something about this dream, there was a divine revelation while I was in the dream the things I saw and heard were so symbolic.

But lately I had been "Seeking Him" I guess you would say. My little sister had started getting deeper into the faith and she would call and pray with me sometimes, and talk about fasting, which I had never done. All in the mean while nobody knew I was feeling lonely in my marriage. It was very frustrating, to the point where I began to just want somebody to talk to. So, I kind of started talking to GOD more, really unconsciously just knowing He would listen, but not expecting Him to do anything about it, let alone reply.

Side Note

Now, my husband is a really nice man. He's gentle kind, patient, friendly, he was just wrapped up in his own world. The more I begged him to spend time with me and I saw no change I began to drift. But everything changed the day I saw this add to get a free copy of the book "Kingdom Marriage" by Tony Evans. I read a brief description of the book and sorrowfully said to myself, "GOD I want a "Kingdom Marriage," and left it at that. My copy came in the mail, and I kept telling myself I would get around to read it, but I kept pushing it off.

    I began to cry out to GOD and asked Him to send me a friend that would spend time with me and give me something to do. It seemed like the only time me and my husband would spend time together is when we were doing things he would like to do. Unfortunately, the friend never came, but I began to get an unshakable desire to dust off the Bible my grandma gave me when I got baptized, 5 years ago and read it. I read a little each day until it became a routine. I didn't know then, but the feeling that started coming over me when I would cuss, smoke, or drink with our friends was "conviction.

    Then one day everything changed. It was a regular day; I was on a trip to the corner grocery store and as I was on my way back home my mother called me and said Kendryana GOD wants to speak to you. Catching me off guard with a statement like that, a smirk crawled across my face. Then, it was my little sisters voice that began to speak with authority, and she called my name, Kendryana! I pulled over and put the car in park and said yes, and she spoke "My Faithful servant If you don't turn from your wicked

Side Note

ways, you will surely perish." I humbly, childlike replied "Ok." Still confused about how all of this came up, it was like my soul knew exactly what was going on. GOD HAD COME TO OUR FAMILY…. He kept urging me to turn from my wicked ways after I had cried out to Him. His words were also confirmation to the dreams, I had been having about me dying, weeks before.

She began to speak about a fast. HE told my family to fast for 3 days fruits and vegetables. We had never fasted as a family before, and only my sister had an understanding. Before this the only fasting, I had ever heard of were the beginning of the year Daniel Fast's that our church held, which I fully never understood what a Daniel Fast even was? I had no clue it was the same Daniel that was thrown into the lion's den! Who knew! Had they said that I might have taken part in it and tried to understand. The only other times were those people who go and live in the jungle to become one with themselves. It turns out these are two totally different reasons for fasting.

So, we all agreed that we were going to obey GOD and fast. Let me tell you it was the hardest thing at the time I had ever done, but it was the most emotional. For those 3 days My sister prophesied, and we wept, and I cried to GOD to spare me, to spare my life. It was like my house was the city of Ninevah and my sister was Jonah. I had never cried so hard for anything before, but the thought of my girls not having a mom, or my husband getting remarried and having to bury me was enough to make me cry until my head was pounding.

Side Note

Until... I finally came on the third day and told GOD in my closet. I said GOD if it's not in your Will to spare my life please let my husband find someone that will love my babies and not mistreat them. I didn't have it in me to ask that she love him, I was ready for that part yet. But I said please if your servant has found favor in your sight, please LORD don't let me die.

The 4th day came, and my sister began to prophesy, and she looked at me and said GOD spared your life Kendryana. The whales of my mother I could barely hear myself think tears began to pour out of my eyes. She said, "the devil is mad, and said that's not fair, and she said she heard GOD say my game my rules." Till this day this conversation lingers in the back of my mind. All of a sudden, she looked up at me again, and called my husband's name who by the way hadn't been a part of this experience GOD didn't tell us to invite him, so it was just my mom, two sisters, and I. She said, He will cheat on you, and I began to cry "Why LORD! GOD said the devil will send a demon disguised as a woman to deceive him. He said it will only happen one time, but woe unto that woman for I will drive a two-edged sword between them. GOD said to pray for her for she does not know HIM. I couldn't stop crying and I said I can't do this, and my sister spoke and said, "I spared your life is it not more than your marriage."

GOD, was indicating that I can do all things If I can spare your life can I not fix your marriage? He also gave me a strict proposition that day. He said, "<u>DO NOT</u> go through his phone and you will continue to love him and let him be

Side Note

the man I called him to be." I said yes LORD. After that I felt cleansed, washed, free, and blessed by GOD. I had never felt so light in my life. My sister prophesied many things Including that I would "Birth" a boy, and GOD spoke through her about each one of us those three days. We praised and worshipped GOD, and our hearts were turned back to the one we had been taught about. But it was like we finally got to meet Him in person.

My journey to loving the one who saved my life had begun!

I wanted to know who this GOD was who had the power to not only speak to me but had the power of my life, in HIS Hands. You see I had never had an encounter like that with GOD. I was raised in the church and knew He was real but just never (until I had an understanding on what It looked like) to have a relationship with Him.

As I began to open my diary to you, As GOD has asked me to share my story with the world, I ask that you please don't judge the secret things of my heart.

Friday July 5th
9:50 am

I fasted for 3 days (July 2,3,4)

Today is the first day after the fast and in these past 3 days everything has never been so clear.

You see JESUS is real! I truly know that now. I know he speaks to me. Little ole me. You see He gave my family a blessing (a changed heart, a sound mind, and a prophet.)
God spoke to me Tuesday May 28th, 2019, He told me that my husband would cheat on me. However, he also told me I was having a boy. I was battling with this news for a while until the day of the gender reveal "June 29th, 2019. When it came out to be a girl. I was discouraged because I really did believe in my heart it was a boy, JESUS told me. Right? It just didn't feel right. However, it was good news because that means that it was just all in my head, and my husband wasn't going to cheat on me. But then God did something miraculous He told me "For I AM God and I "Can not lie" for you are having a boy."

I knew it all along, I let man deceive me I knew I wasn't settled with a girl for some reason. God told me that I shall name him after Nick and his name shall be Nicholas and he shall do great and mighty things.

But wait, the question came back. God, "Is my husband going to cheat on me!?"

God said "Yes." I cried so hard, for I didn't understand. God said, "Do not weep, I need this to happen." He said, "I need to bring Nick so low, that he will call on me." God said, "You see the devil has Nick so low in bondage to him that Nick can't see or hear what's going on, but I have woken you up so that you may see." He said, "A demon disguised, as a woman, sent by Satan will deceive Nick." I cried and cried. I replied, "God why do I have to be at the expense of Nicks salvation. He shouted, in a loud voice, "Humble yourself, your husband is on his way to hell just like you were before I woke you up." He said, "the same way I used your sister for your family salvation, is the same way I'm going to use you for Nicks salvation."

He said He loves Nick SOO, SOOOOO much and he doesn't want him to perish. I said, "Neither do I, but I'm scared it hurts so bad." He said, "I spared your life, why don't you think I will spare your marriage."
I began to cry profusely, He spoke, "Why are you weeping, isn't your life bigger than your marriage?"

I asked God, "Why me?" He said mightily, "Because I said so." He said, "Nick doesn't know me, you do." "I know I can make you strong to bare this weight, Nick can't handle it, if you were the one who cheated." I cried and said, "But God I don't understand.' He said to stop questioning His Will for Nick cheating on me, for it is a blessing. He said this is going to make Nick strong and he will never fall again. God, please give me strength for my heart. My heart is broken and weak. Satan attacks me with images of my husband cheating and it hurts.

God said, "Do not weep child, Satan is a liar, I never told you what would happen."
- I must keep praying and pray hard.
God said, "Woe unto the woman that will try to break up my marriage, for what He puts together let no man separate."
He said, I must pray for her, for she is deceived by Satan? God you must be tripping...
But I understand -_-
God, I'm struggling, how can I pray for someone who will do that.
God said, "You were deceived at some point in your life by the devil before I woke you up." "Pray for your enemies, she will receive the wrath of God."

JESUS HELP ME!!!

Sunday July 7th
8:06pm

    This morning I had a dream, that it was a woman working closely with me and Nick. I don't know if that's true or not it just might be my conscience. I sometimes have flashes in my head of my husband making love to another woman. I stop and tears flood my eyes, and my chest stops beating and I can't breathe. It's not like the anxiety attacks I get when I'm pregnant, it's much worse. It hurts in my heart; I had it happen today. We came from Little Caesars, and I saw my husband having sex with another woman. I was about to cry, but I don't want him to think I'm crazy, so I held it in. He asked what was wrong, but I can't tell him.

    God said to continue to love him and treat him good. I'm trying, I love my husband with all my heart I'm even trying to get him to spend time with me, so I can enjoy him before our marriage falls apart. All I want to do is cry when I see him. I think he thinks I'm too clingy, but I'm just trying to enjoy the happy times.

    I think it will happen in October, a month before I deliver. Can you imagine how I will feel? I'm already going to feel fat and unpretty, and I'm about to bring a newborn baby into the world with my unfaithful husband who I love so much, and then I must bear that pain. It's ok though, some days I'm strong and I'm able to laugh and play with my husband, for I know it will be okay. God said, He's going to work it out for my good. Right now, I'm just trying to put my trust in the LORD, so I can get through this year. GOD said, people will look at me and think that I am "silly" for smiling when my marriage is falling apart. I can't wait until I can smile when it's over, because right now I feel anticipation, anger, sadness, and depression. I know that's just the devil bringing me down.

 -Every night he's busy, I just get sad, I just want to go on a date. I just want to enjoy my husband before he hurts me. I just want to enjoy him while I'm happy, but he's not letting me. He'd rather spend time with everyone else.

Monday July 8th
6:42 pm

God, I have so many feelings.

I feel so broken, I feel like I'm going crazy. I think he doesn't believe it's a boy, but God you said he wouldn't believe until the baby was born. So, I'm going to just keep my thoughts and feelings to myself, so I don't make him uncomfortable.

Please forgive me God, a part of me wishes I didn't believe either. Then the thought of my husband cheating on me would be a lie!!! Then I wouldn't think my husband was cheating on me every time he leaves the house. God, please make me strong. I can't live like this. It's so crazy how one day I go from knowing me and my husband would never do anything like his to each other. To a dream, and now my whole world is crushed.

Tuesday July 9th, 2019

    God woke me up and told me to pray for my husband, that he would meet her soon. God, I'm struggling, today was not a good day.

Thursday July 11th, 2019

God today was a good day. Every time I thought about it or got sad, I said to myself, it's not about me, stop being selfish, God is trying to work on Nick.

It's hard to see it like that, but it keeps me going.
I just pray it will happen soon. Not that I want to be hurt, but this anxiety of my husband cheating on me is tearing me apart and breaking me down. I'm scared, but I know God got me. Thank you God, for not leaving me.

Monday July 15th, 2019,
8:03pm

I feel like I'm drowning, barley coming up for air. Every time my husband's phone rings, or he gets a text message my heart drops. Is it her? Is she sending naked pics? God, every time he hangs up with me is he calling her? God told me to delete my social media, and DON'T GO THROUGH HIS PHONE!
God I'm angry. Why are you keeping me out of the loop?
I just don't want to be made a fool of God. Here I am giving everything I got in my marriage, and my husband can throw it all away.

A part of me wants to believe that I'm making all this up in my head. That my husband could never do something like this because he loves me so much. But unfortunately, I have this strong feeling and I believe GOD. I believe I'm carrying a baby boy; I believe my husband will hurt me. BUT GOD, is working on me for a reason He wants me to have compassion for my husband.
He is showing me that no matter how confidant a man or woman is in their relationship, if they don't have GOD...
The flesh is weak, and the devil can easily deceive them.
I believe that's what happened to Peter in the bible when he betrayed JESUS. It is only through Christ JESUS that we can resist the temptation of the enemy to betray the one we love. Sometimes I pray that my husband won't be a fool and be deceived by Satan, but deep down I know this must happen, GOD wants my husband to believe He's real, I guess the birth of this baby won't be enough. He'll try to put logic with it, maybe saying, "I can feel it because me and the baby are connected. Which is bull crap, the mother of the baby is just as surprised to know the gender like everyone else.

Thursday July 18th
8: 15 am

    I find myself becoming angry each day... My husband hides his phone under his pillow when he sleeps ... Like this man don't sleep through the slaves being freed in the south. If I wanted to go through it, I could.

God, I just want my husband to pray with me when I'm scared and when I'm lost.

 God is it her?... why is he talking to her, she is one of the reasons we broke up when we were younger... God, I'm sorry, but I FEEL LIKE I'M BEING TOTURED. I know all these things, but there's nothing I can do, but sit back and watch my husband hurt me. I'm so lost. I'm sure my husband thinks I'm bi-polar, it's just sometimes, he thinks I'm stupid and it makes me angry... and sometimes I just can't bear to think about the pain I'm going to feel when it happens. I wish my husband knew you God I don't want to go through this.

    I wonder were those JESUS'S thoughts when He knew death was coming, I wish they knew you, Father. I pray they would turn from their wicked ways and seek your face, so I wouldn't have to feel this PAIN. I just want to cry every day; I don't even want to do my hair. I painted the bathroom because it takes my mind off the stress... I feel like everyone is tearing me apart piece by piece... My kids are making parenting challenging, and my marriage is getting stressful.

    LORD, I know you want me to be a better woman, slowly you're showing me how to do things the right way. God, I know your preparing me for what's to come. You said you will make my husband a better man, but I know we must get pass this rough patch of pain.... God keep me so I don't run off with a man that will take away the pain.

Keep me so I don't turn to depression, drugs, weed, or sex to deal with my life.

I'm scared, every day I'm so scared because I DON'T KNOW WHEN MY HUSBAND WILL BETRAY ME. I don't understand sometimes, but the bible says lean not on your own understanding and trust in the LORD. So, I'll keep praying every day through the tears.

I don't want to cause fights and arguments in my marriage. I just need somebody to speak to God. GOD give me peace that surpasses my understanding. I you can and will give me peace and forgiveness in my storm. You will give me an unexplainable peace that never leaves.

How do I get that? What can I do to get that?

God, please carry me... I need you now LORD. I need you now... not another second nor another minute, I can't wait another day. LORD, I need you right away.

Thursday August 8th,
2019, 11:14 pm

Right now, in my life, I'm just focused on my relationship with GOD and everything He wants me to do.
-He wants me to be prepared for my marriage to fall apart.
-And He wants me to have a natural Birth.
-He wants me to work on forgiveness, trust, and study the bible.

For I will find strength in those.

Friday Augst 9th
2019 1:59pm

GOD I'm struggling...

    Today everything was fine. My husband and I were on the phone having a conversation about porn, how we first got involved, it was very engaging, but I guess I got too comfortable. I turned to him looking for support on the subject and all he did was make me feel crazy. I told him of how you recently showed me pornography was a sin. He made me feel like I had a porn addiction, that's why I feel this way. We got off the phone when I asked him when he died, where did he think he was going? He didn't answer. I wasn't testing him, I just wanted to see if he believed in Heaven or Hell.

    God, I don't understand why you would take me through this after I got married, my husband feels like I'm changing on him. I feel like I'm changing myself, but it's that I know better now, and it hurts. I guess this is how My daughter feels when we tell her to stop playing and running in the house. It's not fair when she sees the babies doing it, but they don't know better yet.

God, you answered my question.
I asked why you would change me after I got married?
You said, so my life can be a testimony to my husband. You said, once I clean you up, he would have seen where you came from and know I can do the same for him.
God I'm seeing that it really does hurt being unequally yoked.

Monday August 12th, 2019, 7:17 am

My husband just left for work. God, I feel like I want to cry. Yesterday me and him talked about me wanting to have a baby shower, he said no because then people will bring gifts for a girl. God, I don't feel that you want me to have a baby shower, maybe I'm just being selfish and don't care who does not believe me. But that's not right. I asked to talk to him this morning about the baby shower, to tell him that I agree, I'm not having a baby shower. He told me to go ahead and tell him all my thoughts on why, so I don't interrupt his radio show on his drive to work. So, I began to tell him of the story, you told me God. As soon as I began, and it was about the bible he cut me off and looked at the time and left. It was the most hurtful thing ever.

God told me about the story about Mary and Joseph... How Mary was a virgin and became pregnant, without having "sex" God came to her and told her she would birth the Son Of GOD. Joseph saw her one day and her stomach was getting bigger. Joseph didn't believe her at first, he thought she had been with someone else. "How can you be pregnant without having sex", and then you're claiming to be pregnant with the Son OF God.? God said Joseph had a relationship with me and I still had to send an angel to him to make him believe, so that he would marry Mary. Nick doesn't know me, so why do you keep expecting him to believe you. I said wow God, I know, I'm sorry God please fix my heart. I'm just tired of feeling like I'm crazy. But God I'll be crazy for you.

I know it's only a little while longer, build me up God. I'm sorry I'm not being humble!!

Tuesday August 13th
9:09pm

God my anniversary is coming up. I just want to have a nice time with my husband. I want to forget about all the bad things and just relax. I don't want to be upset, or angry, or unhappy. I just want to enjoy our time together. Too bad I'm pregnant, but it's ok we will still have fun. Man, I want a funnel cake.

Lord, you know I love my husband so much and I never want to hurt him, but sometimes marriage can become a bit overwhelming and sometimes stressful.
God, please give me strength.
Now I know why JESUS told Satan, "Hurry up and do what you're going to do and make it quick.
God I'm praying that you be with me, be my armor and my comforter. Be my tear dryer, and my food when I have no appetite.

Wednesday August 14th, 2019,
7:25pm

God why do I have to wait on my husband to spend time with me.

God help me with parenting. I'm struggling I'm stressed, I'm confused, I'm angry, I'm overwhelmed, God, I'm trying to do everything I can, I'm praying hard for help. I don't understand why they try my patience. I don't understand why they push me to my breaking point.

Please LORD, help me rejoice even when my life is falling apart. Even when times get hard. Help me see the light in my situations.

God, I know pretty is my soul, but my flesh looks disgusting sometimes. I'm getting fat, I'm tired, I barely want to put lotion on. I just feel unpretty a lot. God, please help me. This is hard, I'm so lost God there's so many thoughts going through my head. Why do I have to tell my husband that I want to make love. Why do I always have to make the first move. It's annoying.

Friday August 16th, 2019,
7:45 AM

God, this morning you said when Nick cheats on me I'm going to think it is the most hurtful thing, that has ever happened to me. But you said, I will rejoice because I will look in the mirror and finally see your face looking back at me.

God, how do I digest this and pray for strength about this message the day before my anniversary. How do I enjoy my anniversary, when all I can think about is my husband betraying our marriage. But, God, you told me to rejoice that my husband will finally hear you and see you.

Saturday August 17th
2am

It's my anniversary, my husband didn't come home yet, God, I'm not trying to act like his mother, but you're a grown man I shouldn't have to call and remind you it's getting late. You're married, you're not single anymore. You can't do what single people do.

God, I can't do this you're going to have to pick someone else. I'm tired of this bull... Every time he goes out it's the same thing. God when I go out, I don't disrespect him. I don't come in at all hours of the night because I'm married! God what did I do to deserve this, I'm so hurt, broken, and beat down God, I can't take this.

Happy 1 Year Anniversary!

Saturday August 17th, 2019,
10:00pm

God, I had a really nice time for our anniversary. My husband and I spent the day together. It was so peaceful, and I just felt like we needed some time alone without kids. It was amazing!!!

But the end of the day came, and I started thinking about it again. It just makes me feel like I will never be enough for my husband. God is there somebody else for me. I'm angry, I don't want no other man, but I don't know if I can stand by and watch him break my heart.

God, I know you don't like when I think like this but it's frustrating sometimes to stay positive all day when the thought is there in the back of my head. But God today is my anniversary, so I'm not going to ruin the moment. I'm going to forget about what's coming and enjoy the "Now."

Sunday August 18th, 2019,
1:05am

    GOD, as I lay in the bed and look at my husband, I feel sorry for him, for what's about to happen. He's about to lose his world as he knows it. He's about to lose the trust of his wife, and he's about to lose his partner in life.

Lord I just want to say I see him now, vulnerable to the unknown. But God he's my husband and I vowed for better or for worse. And I don't know when I will heal from this, but I vow to lift him up where he stands to hold his hand in our sorrows. To love him no matter what. I meant it when I said I want to grow old with him.

    God he's going to chew my food for me! I've really got to stop saying that. I will chew my own food in the name of JESUS because I will still have my teeth in old age in JESUS name.

    Now that I have understanding that there's power of life and death in the tongue, I understand why I've been having problems with my teeth, and he hasn't. God, I love him, and I know you love him more. So, I'm getting out of the way LORD GOD so you can fix what's broken.

Thank You God.

Monday August 19th, 2019,
8:08 pm

God, today I have joy in my heart, and I'm not letting the enemy tell me that it's anything other than you CHRIST JESUS.

Thank you for your peace today. Thank you for not forsaking me. Today I will hold to my joy as long as I can. I don't like being sad or thinking about what storms are coming.

Tuesday August 20th, 2019

Today was a good day, I just felt really tired. The enemy tried to attack, but I kept blocking. Thank you, JESUS, for building up my strength, and for giving me peace.

Friday August 23rd, 2019,
8:47 pm

God, I'm praying that you can help me prepare for this. My heart gets really full and heavy sometimes. God help me pray for the days to come. God please be with me when my heart is broken into a thousand pieces. When my breath is gone, and I feel like I can't breathe. When I can't stop the tears from falling. When I don't want to get out the bed and brush my hair, teeth, or wash my face. Give me strength, for my children still need me. Give me strength to still smile and pray for my husband. Continue to please work on me God.

God, I have faith that you're going to work it out, you said watch what I do with Nick. I'm going to have a new husband. Just please GOD help me through the healing process. Help me to not stray away from you or him. God, I get the feeling it's coming soon I don't want to be scared God I want to be ready.

Help me please.

Sunday August 25th, 2019,
8:50PM

     Kendryana, I'm writing this for you. When the day comes that your husband breaks your heart into a thousand pieces, I want you to know these things. When you feel like your world has been torn apart, and you have nothing else to live for. Remember...

 You are beautiful, I love you and God loves you so much< this was not about you, God needs Nick to fall so that he could be the one to pick him up, and not weed, not alcohol, not his friends, not music, not pornography, not drugs, not sleep, not you, but GOD and only Him.

     You are strong, stay with God, HE is right there waiting to rebuild with you. He's waiting for you to fall to your knees and pray and sit back and watch him work on Nick and you. Let him rebuild a Godly Marriage so one day you can get married again to a new man, a new Nick.

Monday August 26 8:19 pm

God, I think the hardest part is going to be watching my husband lie to my face.

The day it will happen God, you said, I will know once it's done, you said you would show me, but not to ask him about it right away because he will lie. God how am I supposed to act knowing my husband has been with another woman. God this is hard. Wow God, I can honestly say your changing me because the old Kendryana would have filed for a divorce already and I would have been looking crazy. God I'm trying to prepare. The devil is working, but God I know your ten steps ahead. And I know you want me to be too.

God, I know you won't stop the tears and the pain from coming, but I know you'll give me strength and peace that surpasses my understanding.

Test and Trials

Wednesday August 28th
12:35pm

GOD, last night my husband wanted to watch this new stand up. I wanted to watch it with him, I love spending time with my husband. But God, you showed me something last night. When the show came on there was a lot of cussing and God at first, I didn't think my mouth was changing, but for the simple fact that it bothered me, means me praying for me to stop cussing is working. I don't even like hearing it anymore. And Lord he started talking about children being molested. The last stand up we watched, the lady was playing with God, and immediately my husband got upset because I told him I didn't want to watch it. Because I realize, that now that I'm walking with you God and living by your standards somethings just aren't funny anymore. I don't even know if I want a pina colada anymore.!!

Nick turned the tv off and put in his headphones in. I wanted to cry, I felt like he just shut me out. And then in that very moment I heard you say...Look this is what it means to be unequally yoked. You guys have different interests now. And it made me so sad I had to go pray. Because the things I loved doing with my husband just weren't me anymore (smoking weed, drinking, watching comedy and tv shows).

These things were making me uncomfortable to be around. And then the question came. Is that why my husband will cheat on me because I won't be relatable anymore? Is that a good enough reason because I'm trying to change my life around?

God, I kept having dreams that I was going back to my last job. In my dream today, you said Satan wants me to go **Back** to my last job so that it would be my escape from Nick.

Satan wants me to go backwards in general, back to everything you delivered me from. He wants this pain to cause me to fall hard.

God, you said if I didn't lead you or tell you it's not Me! Lord, I don't want the thought of my husband cheating on me, to scare me, or make me weak. LORD don't let me do anything that I will regret. Please keep me. Please strengthen me I need you (Abba).

GOD I'm ready for this boy to be born. I hope he brings joy to my husband in his time of need. JESUS, you said pray for the people that don't believe, so that when the boy is born, they will believe in you and your Father

JESUS help me with my parenting. Thank you, I notice I'm getting more and more patient each day. Sometimes I have slip ups but, I'm getting better thank you.

Monday September 2nd, 2019,
10:44 am

Good morning GOD,

    Thank you for waking me up this morning. Two nights ago, I had a dream you were talking to me all night long. You told me to start preparing the right way. You said peace and understanding doesn't just fall upon you. You get it by, reading the word of GOD, and meditating on the Word, praying, speaking to God, and asking for His wisdom. You showed me that if JESUS didn't prepare this way, he would have never been able to bare the weight of the cross and been able to successfully fulfill "HIS" Purpose. You showed me He would have been on the cross hollering and screaming, or worse. What if He had never made it to the cross? What if He hid when Judas came to betray Him? But He was prepared and lived by your ways, mercy, and truthfulness. He gave it to you, a sacrifice pleasing unto GOD.

    You are showing me that when I deliver this baby naturally, and when my husband cheats on me, with the right preparation I will be able to successfully bare my cross, endure the pain, and pray through the storm. Lord, you showed me last night, stop trying to make Nick live your salvation path with you. The things you called me to do are not for him right now.
You told me to stop watching certain shows, not him. You said to just pray for him, that he will see how it corrupts the mind. You told me to stop masturbating and watching pornography, not him. You said, just pray for him, his time will come, pray that he has strength to resist and be obedient.

Saturday September 7th 2019
2:00am

God, being pregnant is a wonderful experience. It is a wonderful thing, but sometimes my husband makes me hate being pregnant. I feel like he would rather masturbate, than be with me. And it's discouraging, because then I don't feel like I can please him because I don't feel or look like the woman he searches for, for pleasure.

God, this makes me so angry, because I feel like this is torture. You want me to stay and love a man that doesn't want me, and that eventually is going to cheat on me. Every day! I don't even know when he's going to cheat on me so every day, I'm hurting. Somedays I'm lonely, some days I'm angry, and somedays I just really don't understand why I must go through this. It hurst God, it hurts really bad.

You said my husband loves me. How? How God? I don't make him feel like this. Sometimes when I get really sad, I just want to run away. I think of how I don't have a car, and how I must rely on my husband. Is that why he's going to take advantage of me and cheat on me? Is it because I have to rely on him. This sucks God. When he cheats, I can't even hop in the car and scream and cry and drive till I run out of gas like you see in the movies. NO!! that won't be me. I can pack my stuff and stand on the curb and wait for an uber driver to come and rescue me from the lies, the hurt, the anger, the pain, and the ugly truth of the man I said I do to.

God I'm hurting.
I've been trying to be strong, but I guess I wasn't doing it right because I'm breaking down.

Saturday September 7th, 2019,
9:27 pm
First, thank you for letting my baby see her 2nd birthday.

Today we went to the arcade. I think everyone really enjoyed themselves. And the cheesecake is amazing.

My husband is getting ready to go to his friend's performance. I'm not sure how I feel. At first, I was angry. I'm tired of staying at home all the time watching kids and taking care of kids while everyone else goes out and lives their best life. I'm tired of my husband not being considerate of me. I get up early every weekend, and for the past two days I got up so early. And now he's going to go out and get up tomorrow at 3pm. I never see him get up on the weekend and take care of the kids while I sleep in.

I was just angry at God.
I felt like my life, was basically me waiting on everyone else hand and foot while people run over me, use me, take advantage of me, and I'm supposed to just take it, be happy… And when I do say something I'm wrong. Well, my throat is heavy, and my tears are flooding. I don't know if tonight is the night my husband will cheat on me, meet her, talk to her. I don't know. But I'm going to give it to God, I can't keep letting this tear me down. I'm not going to worry about anything anymore, I'm not going to even call him. If my husband doesn't call, or check in, or cheats I don't care. God will handle it I'm tired. I'm pregnant and tired. I know God got me he said I don't have to worry my life is in His Hands.
Goodnight!

Thursday September 12, 2019,
11:12 pm

God my husband is "Confident." You showed me today that confidence will be his downfall. You showed me how confident he was in his own strength. He said he would never cheat on me, that it was not even in his mind to do. You said the flesh is weak. We are nothing without God, we will fall short every time if we have confidence in our own selves, and not in God. Just ask Peter, I believe he genuinely did love JESUS, very much. How could you not fall in love with Him, especially when you get to spend that much time with Him so close. And If Peter being a disciple of JESUS did something he said he would never do, who am I.

God, all I can do is pray for my husband because you showed me, he's going to fall hard. And when he does, I'm praying that you will have mercy on him, and allow me to have mercy on him. I love him God, but if he hurts me that will be a challenge. I know you are preparing me for that now….

Thank you, God, I love you.

Tuesday September 17th, ,2019,
8:26pm

Thank you, JESUS, for answering all my prayers and providing so much more.

- Feeding me Your Word

-Financial breakthroughs

-My children with learning and homework help

-Changing my husband around salvation

- A home

-Food

- Safe and healthy delivery

- The men in my family salvation

- Restoration for Nick and his family relationships according to your will CHRIST JESUS

- Peace that surpasses all understanding for my whole family

- The Breath of life for me and everyone I meet

- For saving me just in time

- Good health

Sunday September 22, 2019,
1:24 am

    I was in the shower, and I heard God say, read your bible your storm is coming. I don't know if it's going to happen in October, but God, I need you. I'm pregnant, stressed, tired, depressed. I don't know if I can handle my husband cheating on me at a time like this. God please, what do I need to read. What do I need to pray for? All I can do is thank you for life, food, my family, shelter, grace, mercy, and salvation. I don't want to think about the bad right now Lord. I just want to be happy.

    God my husband doesn't believe it's a boy. I know exactly how he feels I'm not mad or upset. I painted the crib blue today and he got upset, because what if it's a girl? God, I have faith, just please help me. LORD, I can't even go baby shopping with my husband because we're on two different pages, and that's the best part about expecting.

Wednesday September 25th, 2019,
10:11 pm

Dear GOD,

After my husband cheats on me I pray that my heart is right so that I can have mercy on him and not want to leave him or get revenge.

I know revenge is not of you God, you are a forgiving, loving, and merciful. You want me to be like you. I know that you're working on me right now, but I still feel angry sometimes.

Monday October 14th, 2019,
8:18pm

Hey Lord, I haven't written in a while, I've been so consumed with getting ready for this baby boy to come. Between the intense fake scare contractions, prepping for this baby, taking care of the children, and just being pregnant I have been so exhausted.

But GOD I'm back! It's October, this is the month I think it might happen, but Lord you said I won't know leading up to it. So maybe I'm wrong, maybe it won't even happen this year. But Lord, just please keep showing me what to pray for so I can mend my marriage, in a positive way. Have mercy on my husband Lord.

Tuesday October 22, 2019,
9:01 pm

Hey GOD, I've been having so many dreams. I know you're preparing me for what's to come. I think I heard November 4th for my baby's due date, I'm not sure though. I think I'm just ready for him to come, but I'm not due until the 22nd I know my husband will be excited to have a baby born on his birthday. God I'm tired, and I'm trying to prepare, I feel like I'm moving so slow!

Well in other words, October is almost gone, and Nick hasn't cheated yet, so maybe I'm wrong. Maybe it's not October. God, what is half a semester. I'm lost, but I trust you.

Wednesday October 23, 2019,
9:56 pm

GOD... I'm confused I know you don't want me to question your plan for my marriage, but eventually my husband is going to start communicating with another woman, if he hasn't ALREADY. And then eventually he will have an affair. I never saw myself being "the other woman, but I would be. I wish you could just tell me you have a husband for me somewhere that won't hurt me. God, I love my husband, but I already know what it feels like for Nick to break my heart. I don't understand why I must feel it again. God my heart has been broken so many times in my life, there's nothing left. I don't understand why his flesh would even allow him to touch another woman. Lord, I feel so betrayed, I try to be a good wife and take care of our kids. I wash his clothes, I cook and clean, just give me to someone who won't hurt me.

Tuesday November 12th, 2019,
7:25pm

Hey, it's been a while, but guess what, I had my Baby!!!
No, it wasn't baby Nicholas it was a Girl!!

Lord, I don't understand! You said I would give birth to a boy? You said to name him Nicholas. I don't get it. But God your Word says, my timing is not your timing. Lord does this mean I'm having another baby. Me and Nick thought our family was complete.
But God you are the Author of my life, so if I'm having another one then please God, I'm just asking that you please equip us financially, emotionally, mentally, spiritually, and let us still be young! Please in JESUS name Amen.

But anyways, let's talk about this beautiful little girl GOD has given us. She was born November 2nd at 3:12pm. Her name is Aubrey Bleu, her dad named her because her room was blue.

Yes, I was disappointed. Not because it was a girl, but because I know what GOD said and I just felt, and thought it was now! So, it just makes me feel like when is my husband going to cheat on me, four years from now! GOD, I can't take it. Please be with me.

The Wait

Wednesday November 13, 2019,
9:24 pm

Sometimes I wish I had a really close friend to talk to right now. My husband's too busy and I'm hurting, I just need some love right now. Sometimes I just really need a hug. My husband is really good at giving those, they just don't always come at the right time. I get lonely sometimes. GOD, I know that you are waiting to be that really close friend that I NEED. I wish I could hear your voice on the phone. I just need some type of personal interaction. I know you won't judge me. I know you won't tell me how I feel is wrong you'll listen and tell me it will be alright.

November 23, 2019,
10:57 pm

Dear GOD,

    Yesterday was my husband's birthday. I wanted him to enjoy his day I really did, but some way we ended up arguing. Lord, I asked you to put forgiveness in my heart for all the things that had made me angry at one point in time. I guess it is working. Because when I saw the text messages from his ex-last night. I wasn't angry at first. I was kind of upset that it was even there because I know my husband would have been upset if he saw something like that on my phone from one of my exes. That's what made me upset, the fact that he thought that was okay. We're not boyfriend or girlfriend anymore I don't care if it an innocent conversation. You shouldn't even have contact with anyone from your past when you're married. Our levels of disrespect were clearly on different pages. Dealing with things like this makes me feel like I don't know if I want to be married sometimes.

    Don't get me wrong, I love my husband, but I don't like having arguments about things I feel should be common sense.

November 24, 2019,
1:10pm

Dear GOD,

    I'm seeking you in everything I do now please guide in my marriage, in parenting, in my spiritual growth, in my relationship with you, in my financial growth, in my calling. Lord, what is my purpose for being born to my mother and father. What is the purpose for having two sisters, and what is my purpose for having three daughters.

Saturday December 14th, 2019,
11:22pm

Hey GOD, how are you. I haven't written in a while. I just don't know what to say. Right now, I just want my husband to spend time with me. I want to feel like I have a husband and not a roommate.

Lord, I feel as though you want me to be a virtuous wife. A proverbs 31 woman. So, I'm going to fast as I study who she is, and what she is, and how I can change from my wicked ways and be like her.

Wednesday August 26, 2020

Wow..., Hey GOD it's been so long since I wrote to you, it's been more than a year. But even though I don't write I'm learning to talk to you every day. Well first off, I want to start off by saying I had the beautiful Gift that you gave Nick and I November 2nd, 2019.

However, it wasn't baby Nicholas. It was a beautiful baby girl named, Aubrey Bleu Scharschmidt. Thank you, Lord. I love her so much. But God, I am lost about what happened. You said I would give birth to a boy, and I was to call his name Nicholas after his father. LORD, what happened. I feel like everyone thinks I'm crazy now. Unfortunately, I really don't care what everyone thinks. God, you said, your ways are not our ways, you said lean not on your own understanding.

Lord I'm just praying for Nick, I feel like I confused him, maybe I even hurt him. Maybe I was supposed to keep that promise between me and you Lord. Or maybe my heart wasn't right, maybe I wanted to prove everyone wrong so bad that I didn't deserve baby Nicholas. God I'm sorry If my heart wasn't right, but you were still merciful and gave me baby Aubrey LORD. She's a joy to have. Now that I look back, you have always been merciful when you gave me Aiyana and Azya after I disappointed you time and time again.

Well, my husband hasn't cheated yet either. Yet, I have been having many dreams about the woman that will deceive him, "the demon." In my dreams you showed me that she doesn't even want Nick, it's me she's after, or should I say who the devil is after.

It's me he's trying to destroy; he's just using her. You showed me the way she views my husband as disgust and pitiful. She's trying to bring me down. Satan is mad that I'm following you JESUS. He wants to destroy my marriage. But Lord, I'm praying for my children every day. I pray for my husband every day. I'm praying for my marriage every day, and I'm praying for myself every day.

A lot of things have happened since last I wrote. 2020 came and so did a plague. The virus, "covid 19". LORD, I'm not scared because whatever happens you are LORD. You are Alpha and Omega, you will protect your people and lead us out of Egypt, to the "Promise Land." Thank you, LORD.

LORD, you told me to homeschool my babies, two days later the plague hit Georgia. GOD you always lead your people away from destruction. Well, my family is progressing, but I lost my cousin, LORD, please take care of him, I know he's with you. My anniversary came, we didn't do anything, but stay at home and spend time with each other. That's how I like it anyways. LORD, I'm so grateful for my husband. I still have bad days where the enemy tries to attack my mind with thoughts of my husband cheating on me, and it saddens me. Yet LORD, you keep me comforted.

September 2, 2020

Hey JESUS, i want to spend more time with you. So, me and you are having a date tonight. I have prepared the table, and I even made a place setting for you, please come and sup with me.

    I just want to say thank you for joining me. There are so many things I want to discuss with you.

1. Marriage
2. Parenting
3. Taking Care of My Household
4. Taking care of my Body
5. Forgiveness

    LORD, you showed me that I cannot wait for my husband to come and spend time with me. I can spend time with you, you are always waiting for me. GOD, I want to start putting you and JESUS first in my life. JESUS you are my Heavenly Husband, GOD you are my Heavenly Father. You are all these things to me; my provider, my date on a lonely night, my comforter, you are my friend, and the lover of my soul. I love you and I thank you so much for walking with me and holding my hand through the rough patches in my life. GOD you are so good even when you're correcting me. Thanks for keeping me in line, and no it doesn't always feel good, but I need it. I want to keep working on our relationship, I want to build in you LORD. I want you a part of my marriage with Nick, and I want my husband to have a relationship with you so you can be the center of our marriage. I want to teach my children about you so that my household will be built upon your statutes and judgements. All my household will serve you. LORD, I want a kingdom marriage, I want a Proverbs 31-woman lifestyle, and I want to raise my children in CHRIST JESUS. I need you and I can do none of these things without you, so please help me.

Saturday September 5, 2020,
10:45 pm

Thank you, Lord, for all you do, for all your care, and everything you're doing in me.

Father, you're telling us a famine is coming.

Father, you brought me to Ezekiel, I read most of it. I'm in chapter 21, not done yet.

LORD, I'm learning how to be alone. I'm learning how to take the little time I have to myself and give it to you. Instead of running after my husband and asking and making him watch movies or spend time with me. You showed me, I don't need anybody to spend time with me I got you God. I got you, thank you for always being there. LORD, I don't want to put you second, I want to run to spend time with you first.

I love my husband very much. He's not perfect, he sins just like me, and has fallen short just like me. There are things that he does right, like help me with the kids and he gets up and goes to work every day. Lord, thank you for working through my husband helping him provide for us. Thank you God, for all the raises and financial blessings you have given him to be able to support his family.

Thank you, please continue to use him.

Monday September 7th, 2020,
9:12

Hey God thank you for allowing my baby to see 3 years old yesterday.

I can't believe my baby is already three, wow. GOD, this year has been stressful, but so was the last one and the year before that. However, I can honestly say thank you.

God, I need you to fix my heart, please clean my heart out, please clean my mind out, please clean my body out. Sometimes my thoughts, eat me alive. I don't want to have to worry about anything, I don't want to think of negative things, and I don't want negativity around me.

Today I got rid of all the things that I didn't ask you if I could have. Now God, I need you to show me all the people in my life that need to go. Please get rid of them God, please.

Lord is this marriage going to be hard. I need you; I'm scared, I know you didn't give me the spirit of fear. So please take this fear away, please.

Thank you for all your doing in my life, my marriage, my house, my body, my mind, my soul/ spirit.

Father spare all our homes if it's pleasing to you LORD. All my family and friends. Lord I'm praying for all the people I know, and all the people I have ever met. GOD spare us LORD, for what is coming all these sicknesses and rumors of famines and war.

Father, show me how you want me to organize my house, show me if you even want me to stay in my house. Show me how you want me to prepare for whatever is coming, show me a list LORD. Show me a sign, LORD. Show me what to pray for.

My Husband

GOD I should have made this list before I got married, I should have come to you before I got married.

My Husband
- Knows GOD (the GOD of the Bible, the GOD who created the heavens and the earth
- My Husband Loves GOD
- GOD, I want a man that wants me in every way you made him to want me.
- I want a man that can recognize temptation because he carries the HOLY SPIRIT everywhere he goes.
- I want a man that doesn't delight in looking at another woman.
- I want a man that through JESUS CHRIST he has overcome masturbation and pornography.
- I want a man that is not in bondage to lust and perversion.
- I want the man that you called to be my husband to take care of me and my family.
- I want a man that is going to love our children unconditionally.
- God, I want the man you have for me.

- Lord, if you are willing, and if it pleases you, can I have Nick.
- And if yes, please fix him up like you're doing me and make him the man you created him to be.

A Wife - Me As A Wife

GOD, I'm sorry I didn't get a chance to come to you and ask you to make me the wife you created me to be before I got married. I'm sorry I created a marriage before I came to you. I want you to make me a Proverbs 31 woman and give me a Kingdom Marriage.

A Wife
- GOD make me a wife that knows you.
- A wife that has a heart for you GOD.
- Lord, make me a wife that you are pleased with.
- Make me a wife that my Husband is pleased with.
- Make me a wife that won't fall into temptation, because I carry the HOLY SPIRIT
- Make me a wife that only has eyes for her husband.
- Make me the wife you designed and created me to be.

- Father, if it is pleasing to you, can give me to Nick, I love him.

GOD Fix MY Marriage

I'm going to move out of the way, and stop trying to figure, fix, sort, find, look, seek, do, anything, and everything that you did not tell me to do.
GOD change me, while I focus on your word, while I fast and pray.

Tuesday September 22, 2020,
8:09pm

Thank you, Father, for everything. Thank you for my cleaning side work sheets. I love them so much. It's week 2 and the house is clean I'm staying on top of the laundry, and you're delivering me from yelling, cussing, and fusing. You delivered me from this lazy and procrastinating spirit. Thank you, LORD, I'm just praying for order, and that these things that you're doing in me stay. Thank you, Lord, for turning me into a Proverbs 31 woman!

Father help me through this please. I need you to show me my part so that I can be still, stand aside and let you be GOD, and GOD alone. I want to know that you are GOD, I don't want to put you in a box. You are the creator of all things. You are Almighty.

Sunday September 27th, 2020, 2:00am

Papa GOD, when I got married, I didn't have seeing eyes or hearing ears. Also, I know you're changing Nick, like you're changing me. I know Nick's changes are not all done yet or may not have even started but I do see the things I prayed for slowly being removed from him. Basically, what I'm saying is I want to start all over. I want you to show me my husband. Father, you know him better than he knows himself. Show me him father, show me the man I married good and bad, and in the process show me myself good and bad. Show me the man I married his flesh and his spirit. Show me what I need to fast for. Show me what we're doing to our children good and bad. Show me LORD, please Papa. I want to see.

Sunday September 27, 2020, 4:01

      Papa GOD, I feel like my marriage is headed for destruction now that I'm seeking you more and doing all these fast. I see my husband and I growing more and more apart. I know there are things that you don't want me to do with him anymore, that's hard for me to explain. It was very hard for me to explain to him that I couldn't watch one of our favorite shows anymore with him. GOD, I feel so alone, I can't handle all this, but I know you can. I know you're going to keep me sane. Sometimes I just feel like I want him to be saved already. It hurts me with us being on two different pages, I don't want to get hurt anymore GOD, but I know following you means there will be pain, and people will hurt you. Help me to forgive him and others. My heart is hurting.

Monday October 12, 2020, 10:42

GOD, I know you want me to let him go. I know you want me to stop trying to control every situation. I know you want me to stop watching him and stop worrying about when it's going to happen. Or if it's happening now. LORD, I know you want me to stop worrying about if he's looking at another woman or if he's talking to someone else. I know you just want me to pray for him and give him over to you. I know you want me to get out of the way and let you handle him. GOD surrendering is so hard, but I know that when I truly and finally get out of the way you will began to move supernaturally because you fight my battles not me. GOD help me throw the towel in and completely get out of the way. LORD, I love him, but I want to love you more. And with loving you more, it means that I believe you. I believe that you are going to tear down this marriage that Nick and I tried to build ourselves and give us a real one. You're going to give us a marriage that no woman, no demon, no Satan, no dog, no cat, or no man can tear apart. I'm going to keep praying and fasting for my marriage, family, children, myself, strength, household, and everything the HOLY SPIRIT leads me to fast and pray for. Thank you Lord, I love you.

Tuesday October 13, 2020,
11:37pm

LORD, thank you for my husband. Papa, I know we both were not children of GOD when we met so I'm not sure if you chose him or I did. However, I'm so happy you allowed me to marry him. LORD, I want to erase everything in my mind about marriage that I see on tv, cartoons, lifetime, the internet, and the world in general. Even what i saw in my parents. Father, I want you to teach me about marriage. Show me what it means, and what it is. Show me what a "wife" is and how to be one. Show me what a "husband" is and how to submit to one. What are the roles? So, LORD I'm praying this prayer.

Papa GOD, make me Nick's "Eve" and make Nick my "Adam." Shape me from his rib, make me his help mate, but please I pray that you make us both strong enough to fight off the temptations of the enemy. In JESUS name Amen.

GOD who better than to come to about marriage than the creator of it.

Tuesday November 3rd, 2020, 9:29pm

I'm starting to realize that everything I ever wanted and needed, you are. That's why you are I AM, because you are everything I need. LORD, when I want to cuddle, can you be my cuddle buddy, and when I'm hungry, can you feed me. Father, I'm not scared because I have you. The bible says your name is a strong tower, that I may run to it for protection and safety. I want to talk sometimes, is it ok if I call you. But Father I don't want to be a selfish companion, what do you want. Are you happy, are you sad, what's on your mind. DO you want to talk Father? Do you have a favorite color, or are you all the colors? There's so much I don't understand, but that's ok, that's why you make a good talking buddy/ teacher. Thers is so much for me to learn from you LORD, you make a good everything. Thank you, Father, for healing me. I love you.

Wednesday November 4th, 2020,
9:50

I am better off now than I was!!
GOD, My First Father, My creator found me in my mess.

He found me out in the wilderness wandering around in the dark with chains bound around my neck and hands. I was running out of time, and death was coming for me. I was a child of Satan in bondage doing things that were not of GOD, sinning and sin leads to death.

But my creator used my sister to come and call our family out of the dark to give me another chance. He spared my life. After a 3 day fast, he told me that he was going to spare my life. He adopted me, now I belong to the Father in Heaven. The GOD of love, the GOD of Abraham, Isaac, Jacob, and mosses. The Father of JESUS CHRIST of Nazareth. He found me, a sin junkie, dirty, beaten, stinky, rotten, empty, dead, abused, and misused. He found me, brought me to His well of living water and gave me a drink. And when He did that, my eyes were then opened. Then He gave me a bath. He slowly washed away all my iniquity. As I stepped back and watched what He was doing I saw real love. He didn't judge me, he didn't ask where I had been, or what I had done, or been doing. He wasn't afraid to touch my filth. He kissed my wounds and healed them. He made me new and clean. He showed me kindness, love, and affection. Thank You, Thank You JESUS for what you've done for me. Thank you, thank you, thank you, thank you, thank you. You made me alive. I was born dead, in the dark and scared, but you came and cleaned me up and turned on your lights and told me I didn't have to be scared anymore. Thats what it means to be saved.

Thank you for loving me. I know who's I am, my Father is wealthy, He owns everything, the whole world and everything in it. He is I AM; He loves me.

He's nobody to play with. He's mighty, mightier than anything you've ever seen, but He's so sweet, sweeter than honey, and He's fair. He's Holy. There is no other Daddy like Him, and that's a fact!

Sunday November 6th, 2020,
9:10

LORD thank you! For allowing me to see that man can't do anything for me. That, it is you who makes me feel better, during times when I'm sad, lonely, sick, down, and depressed. It is you who fills me up. Man's kindness only lasts for so long until it doesn't benefit them anymore. But GOD!! Your kindness will last forever. LORD, make me like you so that I can show the same type of kindness to my husband, my children, my mother, my sisters, to family, to friends, and to strangers. LORD, I want to be like the good Samaritan, but I want to be led by you. Thank you for showing me people's hearts. Please tell me what to do next.

The Sabbath

I have sinned against the LORD today.
I'm sorry Father.
I did not honor the sabbath, like He asked me to. I cussed on church grounds, I put on makeup, after you told me not to. I let the cares of my feelings/ heart get in the way of God's Day. I did not delight in GOD today. I did not pray and spend time with you Father. I watched things that were unpleasing to GOD. I did not fast, and I did not keep the way of the Lord.
I read a scripture that Jesus said, He said if you love me. Then keep my commandments. Why do we get upset when our children don't do what we have asked them to do or not to do, but we take your commandments lightly Lord? I'm sorry.

Sunday November 22, 2020,
8:05pm

GOD today is my husband's birthday.

    God I just don't know,
Lord this is hard. Being unequally yoked is hard. This is a heavy burden, please stop the attacks. Please call off the attacks. I'm praying for my husband LORD, please help me!! I just don't know; I feel like I'm headed for the drop off. I'm struggling LORD, I'm struggling hard. How do I get by GOD, how do I get by, I feel like I'm doing life alone. I feel like the pressure of the kids is all on me, but thank you for Nick, he's doing an awesome job. I'm still praying for him; I know he's doing the best he can. Please help me keep standing and stay quiet through the attacks.

Saturday January 2nd, 2021,
2:59am
Happy New Year LORD!!!!

Thank you so much for allowing me to get off the boat in this new year! LORD, I ask humbly to please heal me this year, deliver me this year, and save me this year. Keep my children their whole life, keep my husband, his whole life, keep my fathers, my sister, and mothers, aunts, uncles, cousins, my niece, friends, grandparents, other relatives, and those in my neighborhood.

LORD JESUS, KING JESUS, continue to deliver me please from everything I'm struggling with and help me to surrender to you LORD.

Sunday January 3rd, 2021, - Wednesday January 6th, 2021,

The book of Esther... If I perish, then I perish.

I fasted.
Four days, and no food. The HOLY SPIRIT kept me.

Friday February 5th, 2021,
7:55am

Good morning, Father, please forgive me for my ways. Father, deliver me from everything Satan is going to try to use to get me to crack. Deliver me from everything Satan is going to try to use to push my buttons.

LORD GOD, Deliver from,
- Offense
- The spirit of aggressiveness
- The spirit of low self esteem
- The controlling spirit
- The spirit of wrath and anger
- The spirit of depression
- Loneliness and emptiness.
- Doubt, always trying to make it happen on my own.
- Deliver me from pain!
- Deliver me from the checkup spirit.
- Deliver me from disobedience.

AND give me LORD,
- Peace, that surpasses all understanding.

And teach me LORD,
- My weapons are not carnal.

Trust the Process

This is for me. GOD is saying…

1-GOD will never permit the righteous to be moved.
Psalm 55:22
·Continue to seek Him in righteousness with your whole heart, and He will never allow us to be moved from Him. In JESUS Name, Amen.

2-GOD is transitioning me out of the old man, and into the newness of the creation of CHRIST JESUS. It's a process that He takes us through to get to our full potential in CHRIST, our destination in HIM. He's shedding off the old man, He's breaking the characteristics of the old man, and cleansing us, purifying us, and sanctifying us into a new creation.

3-We have friends that are walking with us, who do not know the new creation. They can only identify with the old man, who is about to soon be crucified completely. They do not want to come with us on our road to righteousness. The friends I have will depart from me before I begin my trials and tribulations. God is removing people from your life because they're not meant to be carried into this new creation, this new season of life. They're not equipped, they don't want Him, they don't seek Him. They will talk to you about Him, but they don't want HIM. They are dead weight, and you have to let it go. When you let them go the purification process begins. GOD is trying to take you higher.

4-Endurance, perseverance, humility through this process GOD is taking you through, you will be humbled, and you will have to endure until the end. Having patience, don't try to rush the process. Do not try to speed ahead of the LORD, 1 step at a time. People are going to see this change. People are going to witness what's taking place. But this is not a time to be ashamed. People can see the light on you, in you, you will not be able to hide it.

5-Along the way to being tried and tested, there are going to be people who will not like you for no reason. They will expose themselves. Pray for them and keep pushing. The LORD will deal with them, but you stay focused on GOD. GOD will be there at the darkest point in your life. He will always be there.

6-You are going to see people with bigger, better, and nicer things. Do not indulge in it, stay focused.

7-Be slow to wrath, be slow to speak, be wise with your words. This is the season of preparation to enter the new season. He's breaking people off of you. He's destroying some relationships. He is putting you through some test to test your faithfulness. To test how you would react when you are in certain predicaments and situations. Will you depend on Him for everything in your life? Will you put him first?

-Remember even the teacher is silent during the test.
·GOD is not going to always allow us to feel His presence. He wants to see how we will react. Will we fall? Will we be weak, or will we be strong?

8-Take your time, don't feel like you need to rush to get it over with. Take your time and learn from the process, let it teach you. No matter who is looking at your struggles, don't get embarrassed, and don't get down. Don't let that be the reason you want to stop.

9-The moment you rush is the moment you become unbalanced. It's the moment the enemy uses to knock you off track because you weren't stable. Be still and trust in the process and take your time. He will not let you fall, if you stumble, he will be there to make sure you don't fall. His mercy will catch you and hold you up.

Monday February 15th, 2021,
12:30am

I'm laying here watching my husband sleep, and GOD has just given me a revelation of my husband's state. The more and more I get closer to GOD Satan will use people close to me to attack me.

If I don't keep praying for my husband Satan will try to use him like a puppet, but I bind and rebuke that in the Mighty Name of JESUS.

-Pray for him," says the LORD. Satan will deceive him. Nick is not the enemy, I know it will hurt, but pray for him because Satan is trying to destroy him in the process.

Sunday February 21, 2021,
8:32 am

Last night I was talking to Nick about letting go and giving GOD our marriage. I told him I'm not going to ask him about going on a date, him spending time with me, or nothing, anymore. I have given it to GOD!!! So, he started speaking and I didn't even realize it was the HOLY SPIRIT speaking through him to me. I understood though, and I'm so happy GOD did it that way because I needed a word. I needed to hear from you JESUS. Thank you! Nick was saying sometimes you must let some people go, because people are hindering you, and blocking you from your true purpose. Some people are in the way of you unlocking your true potential, and sometimes things must happen for you to see your true potential, even somebody's death. He said not in a bad way but sometimes a person's life was hindering someone from unlocking their true potential.

I understand JESUS.

Wednesday March 17th, 2021,
12:05

LORD, As I'm writing this I'm crying, because I'm so thankful that you're the only one who won't leave me, leave me hanging, leave me lonely, leave me afraid, leave me by myself. You'll always provide. LORD, I don't want to put anyone before you. Thank you, LORD, for loving me.

AND thank you, JESUS, for dying on the cross for me, nobody could have done that for me.

Friday April 9th, 2021
7:32 am

LORD, it's been a long time since I wrote in my Journal concerning what's going on. I've been getting closer to you and have been recording my many dreams.

-Well let's back up on my journey. You taught me about soul ties and demons that are introduced through sexual relationships and other things that come along with sexual relations with another person. The spiritual baggage you exchange when you are intimate with someone. So, LORD on my journey I heard you say refrain from having sex with your husband. I was flabbergasted. I wanted to make sure I heard you right. My response was LORD how am I going to tell him that. And then I asked you to make a way. which gave me a week to figure out what to do after that. Well, I kept slipping by him all the way through February. However, in March I was in the room getting dressed and he grabbed me, and I played it off as if I was trying to get our 1-year-old out the room, and he snatched me back and said "no!" "I'm starting to get pissed off with your games" and he laughed when he said it, but I knew he was serious.

He was slowly unfolding emotionally and mentally, and I was blossoming emotionally and spiritually. I didn't know what to tell him. LORD, it's getting hard to stay focused, I know you are delivering me from things, and I know you don't want me to go back to them. I don't want to go back, but I love my husband, and I know he's falling apart. So yesterday, he finally said we need to talk!!! I already knew what it was about, I hadn't let him touch me since January. And GOD, you recently told me to start sleeping in the kid's room.

So, he said "Kendryana, why I can't I touch on you?" "Do you know how frustrated I've been, it's so hard to stay away from you." "I've been trying to give you your space but."

To Be Continued

Made in the USA
Columbia, SC
18 May 2024

1905fca8-976d-4961-9c1e-78fbc05e72f7R01